Joan Germann Lewis

A Nature Journal

Joan Germann Lewis

Poems by Bernie Lewis

A NATURE JOURNAL
January 2000

All rights reserved.
Copyright ©2000 by Joan G. Lewis

For information e-mail:
bern@azstarnet.com

ISBN 0-9677024-0-2

PRINTED IN THE UNITED STATES OF AMERICA

West•Press
Tucson, Arizona

ACKNOWLEDGMENTS

I want to thank Dr. and Mrs. Paul Dufton of England who were the first to suggest that I do this book, and who sent a copy of *The Country Diary of an Edwardian Lady* by Edith Holden to inspire me. Thanks also to Diane and Ian Thomson, my sister and brother-in-law, for their enthusiastic support. Their gifts of beautiful leather notebooks with blank pages required something special. Alyce Jones deserves my gratitude for consistently urging me to complete this journal here in Green Valley, Arizona, where so many diversions interrupted this project. Some of the diversions, especially art workshops conducted by Eva Briggs, were of enormous benefit. Dick Walton of Concord, Massachusetts, very kindly identified some of the dragonflies and damselflies from photos that I took around the pond and fields.

My deepest thanks go to my husband, Bernie, who brought me to his wonderland, where he shared my enthusiasm and awe for the ever-changing landscape and the lives of the creatures who dwelled or visited here. As an artist, writer and photographer himself, he helped me immensely by critiquing my artwork and writing. He taught me the various uses of cameras which enabled me to photograph the smallest mosses and wildflowers to distant wildlife.

Introduction

In 1970, my husband Bernie bought an abandoned house on 25 acres in northeastern Pennsylvania. Over the years, he rebuilt the house, planted trees, blueberries, vegetable gardens, and dug a pond adjoining a trout stream. He built the barn using hemlocks taken from the pond area. His poems, included in this journal, reflect his love of the land and all living things.

I wish I could include a map large enough to show exactly where the Spring Beauties grow at the edge of the Hemlocks, where Purple Trilliums pop up at one end of the property and Painted Trilliums at the other, where Yellow Violets hide on the banks of the stream and Common Blue Violets grow in the middle of the path above the road.

When I moved here, I wanted to get to know every inch of the property. I searched every nook and cranny; and, in so doing, discovered enormous varieties of mosses, lichens, ferns, fungi, bushes and trees in addition to the fantastic array of wildflowers that appear and disappear within a month or two.

The abundance of wildlife ~ from insects, spiders, birds, amphibians, reptiles and fish to small and large mammals ~ increased my interest and enlarged my portfolio. Soon I was taking notes on all events month by month.

The more I looked, the more I found. It astonished me that I had walked by so many wondrous things only to discover them when my efforts to paint them led me to seek and find. I have never been able to decide which was more enjoyable ~ the Search, the Research or the Painting.

This Nature Journal is a result of this labor of love.

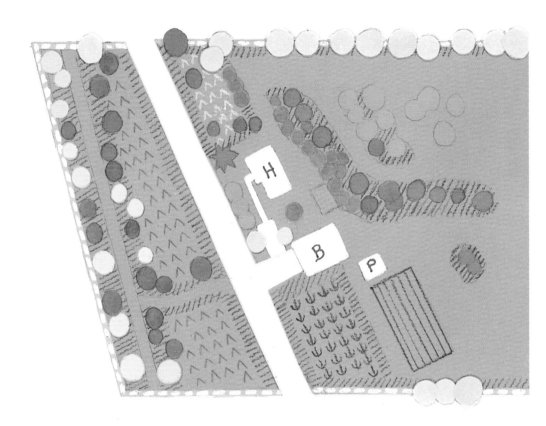

Stone Walls		Red Spruces	
Thickets		Blue Spruces	
Maples		Norway Spruce	
Other Deciduous Trees		White Pines	
Road		Scotch Pines	

NORTHEASTERN PENNSYLVANIA

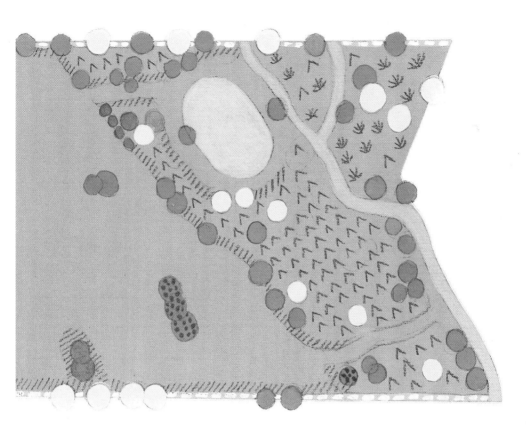

House	H	Tamaracks	●
Blueberries	▦	Apple Trees	◉
Barn	B	Hemlocks	∧
Potting Shed	P	Marsh	↯
Garden	▥	Pond and Stream	□

4

JANUARY

Shadows on the bright snow,
Leaves whisked by the wind,
Scratching against the crust
As they blow.

Trees crushed by white cotton,
Burdened by beauty,
For now by sun and wind
Forgotten.

                    - B. L. L.

Jan. 2 ~

Just as I focused the indoor
camera on a squirrel and rabbit,
a blue jay flew into the scene
surprising us all.

Jan. 4 –

We rarely see deer in the daytime
during the winter. Snowmobiles
must have roused this trio . . .
and we were the final straw.

We seldom saw a Downy Woodpecker until we put out a suet feeder. Now we have a frequent visitor. The Downy is the smallest of the woodpeckers, and the most common woodpecker to visit winter feeders.

Downies are found all over the U.S. except in the Southwest. Some migrate, but most are year-round residents. Insects make up three-fourths of their food; fruit, seeds and sap the remainder.

In winter they can be found in loose flocks with nuthatches and chickadees in mixed coniferous-deciduous forests. In late winter they begin to mark their territory by loud, rapid bursts of drumming with their beaks.

Woodpeckers nest in tree cavities which both male and female excavate. 4-6 white eggs are laid in a chip-lined nest. The male does most of the brooding. The young hatch in 12 days, and are dependent for almost 3 weeks. In the north only one brood is raised.

Downy Woodpecker

A male Cardinal is a daily visitor to the A-frame feeder, first to come and last to leave. Even when all seeds have been devoured, he stays inside the covered feeder surveying his domain. This year, so far, there is no mate to be seen.

The Cardinal is one of a number of southern birds that have extended their ranges northward this century. Others are the Mockingbird, Tufted Titmouse, Mourning Dove, Red-bellied Woodpecker and Turkey Vulture.

Around mating season you can hear the male begin a song and the female complete it a little distance away. Nests are made in thickets where 2-4 eggs are laid which take 2 weeks to incubate. Both parents feed the young. While the female sits on a second clutch of eggs, the male feeds her and the fledglings insects. In our section of the country they will raise two broods by mid-September.

Cardinal

At the Feeders

Jan. 10 ~ Four pairs of
Evening Grosbeaks
came to the feeders
at noon, but
stayed only
5 minutes.
The females
fed on the
ground, the
males at the
hanging feeders.

Jan. 26 ~ 31 Evening Grosbeaks landed
in the uppermost branches of
the wild cherry tree, stayed
15 minutes, then flew south.

They used to breed only in western Canada; now
they breed as far southeast as Massachusetts.
In the winter of 1889~1890 they came to New
England in droves. Lately they've been migrating
as far south as the gulf states.

Eight

Known for their voracious appe-tites, one Evening Grosbeak was reported to have consumed 100 sunflower seeds in less than 5 minutes. Fortunately for other birds they come to feeders irregularly. Favorite foods are seeds of maple, ash and box elder. Their large, sharp-edged beaks are good tools for plucking buds, flowers and fruit.

Nests are generally built in spruce trees from 20-60 feet above the ground where 3~4 eggs are laid.

Evening Grosbeaks

On January 10 around 4:30 in the afternoon, I noticed 10 Mourning Doves roosting in the higher branches of the tallest black cherry tree. As days progressed, more and more doves gathered half an hour to an hour before sunset, then peeled away into the spruces.

On a sunny but cold afternoon (32°), January 21, I counted 60 doves roosting in the cherry trees between 4 and 5 o'clock. They don't appear on days that are foggy, windy, rainy or snowy.

Mourning Doves will winter in the North if the food supply is sufficient. They eat weed seeds, grain and corn in the fields. At bird feeders, they like millet, sunflower and canary seeds.

In their northern range, they breed from April through August. They build flimsy nests 5-25 feet above the ground. 1-2 eggs take 2 weeks to incubate. The young are fed regurgitated "pigeon milk" and later on regurgitated seeds. They raise 3-4 broods a season.

Sixty Mourning Doves

A winter dawn, ablaze with fiery tones
    from orange to gold,
Won't faze the snow-packed land,
    the freezing cold.
But as we gaze at first light's
    brilliant show,
We feel a warmth: the vivid rays
    have energized the snow.

FEBRUARY

Sunrise: 7:15   Sunset: 5:20

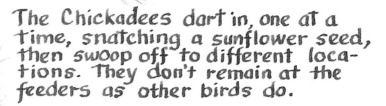

The Chickadees dart in, one at a time, snatching a sunflower seed, then swoop off to different locations. They don't remain at the feeders as other birds do.

A Chickadee will hold a seed with its foot while it hammers it open.

Like the Nuthatch, it can hang upside down on a small twig to get food. Wintering birds eat berries, conifer seeds, insect eggs and pupae. In summer they eat insects, seeds and berries.

At the end of summer they form small flocks which last until they break up into breeding pairs in spring. Both sexes chip out a hole in a stump or tree of partially rotted wood. The female lines the nest with moss, plant down, feathers, fur and cocoons.

Ten to Twenty

5-8 eggs are laid,
one each day, and
are incubated for
12 days. Nestlings
are fed caterpillars.
One or two broods
are raised each
year. Most Chick-
adees mate for life.
Their life span is
about 7 years.

Black-capped Chickadees
are year-round residents
in regions as far north
as Alaska.

Black-capped Chickadees

At the Feeders

The House Sparrow, or English Sparrow, is not a sparrow but a weaver finch transplanted from England to do battle with cankerworms.

Besides battling worms they fight each other (male against male, female against female), attack other birds, snatch their food away, destroy their eggs and usurp their nests. Often they will oust bluebirds or martins from birdhouses and move in.

At the feeders they're fairly peaceful, but exceedingly skittish, constantly darting for cover in the big spruce tree.

When they do build their own nests, they use grass or hay and line them with feathers, meanwhile robbing each other of nesting materials. 3-7 eggs are laid; incubation is 11-13 days. The young are fed insects, at first by regurgitation. They raise 2-5 broods a year.

House Sparrows form large communal roosts at night and smaller roosts during the day. They may travel up to 4 miles to join the roost at night. Around midday smaller groups will gather to preen and chatter. We hear them chirping noisily in the spruce next to the feeders.

Two Dozen Sparrows

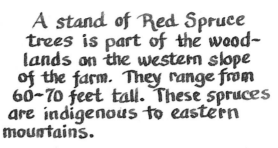

A stand of Red Spruce trees is part of the woodlands on the western slope of the farm. They range from 60~70 feet tall. These spruces are indigenous to eastern mountains.

Spruce cones disperse winged seeds, and mature in one season.

Scotch Pines, now about 40 feet tall, were planted many years ago, extending from the barn to the southern edge of the farm.

All pine cones take two years to mature. The cones open and release their seeds in autumn.

This pond was once part of the Hemlock forest surrounding the stream. Bernie had the area dug out to allow underground springs and a tributary of the stream to fill it to a depth of fourteen feet. He then used the uprooted Hemlocks to build the barn and potting shed.

Hemlock cones mature in one season and disperse seeds on dry, cold days in autumn.

The winter snowfalls have piled up to produce a beautiful wonderland. But February is a critical time of year for deer. Death by starvation is common. Toward the end of February and first half of March, those deer who lose more than 30% of their body weight will succumb. Fawns are greatly at risk since they aren't tall or strong enough to walk through deep snow or compete for forage food at tree branch heights.

In winter, White-tailed Deer in these parts are reduced to browsing on buds, twigs, leaves and shrubs. They prefer hemlocks, yews, white cedars, mountain ash, dogwoods, maples, willows, poplars, cherries and oaks. Spruce, tamarack, mountain laurel and rhododendron are starvation fare. We discovered that the hard way when we returned from a trip in February to find our rhododendrons devoured.

The deer above was in our backyard, reduced to browsing on spruce, more starvation fare. Deer, like cattle, are ruminants, cud-chewers, with four-chambered stomachs that are needed to process large quantities of low-nutrient food.

This deer could be a doe or a buck. Antlers are shed in autumn after each rutting season. They begin to grow in spring with live tissue called "velvet". In fall this dies and strips away leaving hard bony weapons that bucks use to fight each other for possession of does.

Few deer live to their potential life span of 11-12 years; bucks average 1½ years, does 2½-3. But Whitetail Deer are extremely prolific. In spite of deaths due to disease, starvation, hunting, dogs, cars and trucks, their numbers are balanced by annual fawn births which increase herd size by 20-30%.

A SNOWFLAKE

A snowflake fastened to my window,

A luminescent

form limned by

brooding spruce

boughs and

whirlwinds of snow,

Out of teeming sky-formed crystals,

Out of an Olympian crystal factory

Where Vulcan and Ceres combined

To produce infinite and unique

Varieties, no one like any other.

-B.

MARCH

With the deep snows reduced
   to small patches on north slopes,
And the runoff diminished
   to a minor flood,
I hike down to see how the stream
   came through the winter,
And get a few trespass notices posted
   for the start of fishing season,
Only to find huge Hemlocks
   which for decades have withstood
   the ferocious spring freshets,

Tumbled in tangles no colony
   of beavers could ever reproduce,
Undermined by the abrasive water,
Or snapped like toothpicks
   by some stupendous force,
Snapped down over the best
   fishing holes.
The stream has altered so much I fear
The poachers won't recognize it this year.

                             – Bernie

March 15 ~

These nocturnal foragers have
thrown caution to the winds.

At midday we watched deer
grazing on pastures recently
uncovered by melting snow.

At the same time these two
raccoons spent an hour consuming
every edible bit of the kitchen
scraps just added to the compost
pile.

When the snow melts, the only green showing among the detritus of the forest floor comes from clubmosses looking like low-growing conifers, but not even a foot high.

These are miniature replicas of a prehistoric landscape. The great spore plants of ferns, clubmosses and horsetails towered 50 to 100 feet high, flourishing 250 million years ago, long before seed plants developed.

Clubmosses are <u>not</u> mosses. They have woody stems, cells that conduct water, and propagate mainly by creeping along the ground. Spores are produced in cones or "clubs," but rarely germinate.

Mosses, on the other hand, do not have water-carrying pipelines, and reproduce by means of spores.

Shining
Clubmoss
3-6"

Tree Clubmoss
4-7"

Running
Cedar
5-10"

Ground
Pine
4-10"

Mosses and lichens may have been the first plants to live on land. They are most in evidence in early spring after the snow melts and before weeds and wildflowers sprout.

Lichens and mosses act as soil makers. They colonize rocks, fallen trees and barren ground. Then, as they capture wind-borne particles and water, their hosts begin to disintegrate. The released minerals plus the organic matter resulting from the decay of lichens and mosses combine to create a mix that can nourish higher plant forms.

Mosses are always green, always leafy, and usually grow densely packed in low mats or cushions. Life begins with a spore. Usually one plant is a male and another female. Sperm cells need water to reach the top of female plants. When united, a stalk will grow topped with a spore-containing capsule. Spores are released when conditions are just right.

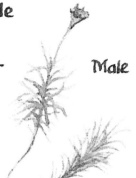

Male

Haircap Moss, or Pigeon Wheat

Female

Purple Moss, or Burned Ground Moss (Mature with Spore Cap)

(Leaves huddle close to stem when dry and open at right angles to stem when wet.)

Ladder Lichens

British Soldiers, or Red Crest Lichens

Lichens come in all colors; they can be crusty, stalked, branched, or shaped in loose folds. They are part fungus, part alga. The fungus anchors the partners and absorbs minerals and water. The green alga makes food for both by photosynthesis. Lichens multiply by fragments breaking away from the original.

36

March —

3 — 20°, deep snow. At the feeders: Redpolls, Blue Jays, Chickadees, Nuthatches, and the male Cardinal.

9 — Seven Deer grazed in meadow where underground seeps melt the snow. They pushed each other away from food sources using their front hoofs.

11 — 40°. At the feeders: 10 Juncos, a Fox Sparrow, Song Sparrow, Purple Finch, Brownheaded Cowbird, Downy Woodpecker and Nuthatch.

13 — An Osprey perched in the Aspen tree near the house until chased away by a Crow. 5 PM: Counted 14 Deer crossing snow-covered field.

15 — At noon, we watched 2 Raccoons forage in our compost pile, while 6 Deer browsed on Big Red's field. Male Cardinal is singing from top branches of Larch. Heard 1st Robin.

17 — 34°, sunny. A female Cardinal showed up at feeders. Pond totally covered by snow.

19 — 45°, rain. 7 Wild Turkeys walked up north meadow into White Pines. Male and female Redwinged Blackbirds came to feeders.

21 — 10° at 7 AM, sunny. Snow on fields half gone. Ice shelves 6-12" deep on sides of stream. Woodchuck in N. meadow. 2 male Evening Grosbeaks came to feeders.

24 — Freezing rain. Everything ice-covered.

26 — 60°, sunny. All snow melted except on pond. Stream very swift, overflowing banks. 2 dozen Robins on lawn by 7 PM.

Song Sparrow   Purple Finch   Dark-eyed Junco   Fox Sparrow

Female Cardinal   Brown-headed Cowbird

Downy Woodpecker   White-breasted Nuthatch

Common Grackle   Robin

27– Snowed most of day. Male Cardinal feeding female in Dogwood bush. A large Common Grackle came to feeders.

31– 40° 8 AM; 58° 2 PM. Stream is down to normal. Most of ice melted on pond. An 8-10" Turtle swam underneath ice cover. Found Turkey feathers and bones of small animals in Pine-Maple grove.

APRIL

There is mystique in nature
In the overwhelming secrets
    of growing things,
In the sad-sweetness
    of seasonal change,
In the song of a bird,
In the enigma of knowing,
    yet not knowing,
What causes
    all this
        to happen.
        ~Bernie

Red Maple pollen flowers

    Purple Finches and House Finches have been coming to the feeders since mid-March, and will stay all summer. The females lack any red or orange coloring. 5½ - 6½"

April 8 — The catkins on this
   aspen lured a flock of Pine Siskins
here on their way north. The bird feeders
induced them to prolong their stay.
We've seen two dozen come for niger
seeds in the morning, but flocks of 50 –
200 are common in the winter. Then it's
a sight to see each tip of a spruce branch
topped by a Pine Siskin.   4½ – 5¼ "

April 12— Here in the Endless Mountains
we can always count on one or two
snowfalls after the daffodils bloom.
And then the Goldfinches arrive. We
watched three pairs come daily to the
feeders for sunflower and niger seeds.
4½ – 5½"

April 12 ~ Tiny, pink-striped Spring
    Beauties are the first wildflowers to
    appear, growing in patches here and
    there near the hemlock woods.

April 18 ~ Yellow, drooping Trout Lilies
    have started to bloom in the woods
    and meadows. Called "trout" because
    of a likeness in the leaf markings to
    those of the brown or brook trout.

April 23 ~ White-throated Sparrows and
    tiny Chipping Sparrows are
    now foraging under
    the feeders and
    in the woods.

This decaying hemlock log is becoming a nursery for a new generation of trees, shrubs, ferns, wildflowers and weeds.

Boring beetles make tunnels in the wood, and to these openings come slugs, woodlice, spiders, centipedes, fungus spores and water.

Then lichens, mosses and fruiting fungi attach themselves to the softened surface, while wood-boring insects and larvae pulverize the interior.

Molds and bacteria complete the process, and the log becomes soil again, enriched by animal and vegetable decomposition.

Hemlock Seedlings

Beech Seedlings

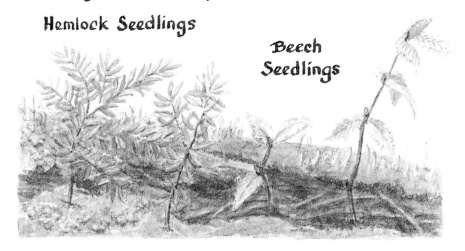

Lichens and Mosses on the Log—

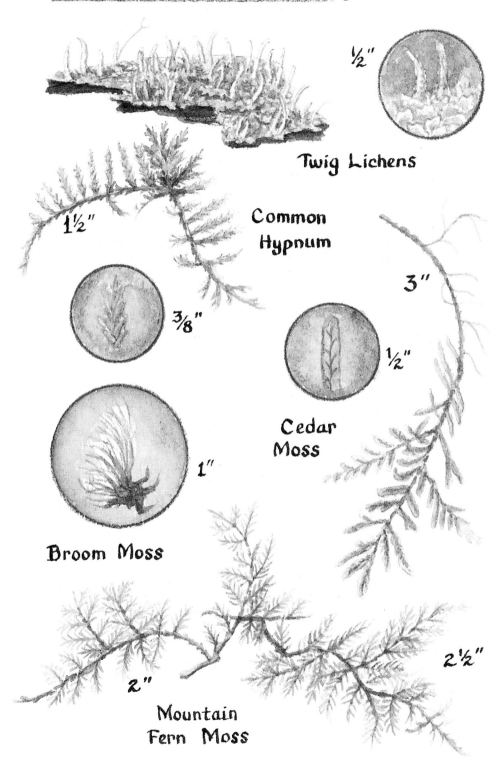

½"

Twig Lichens

1½"

Common
Hypnum

3"

⅜"

½"

Cedar
Moss

1"

Broom Moss

2"

2½"

Mountain
Fern Moss

On and Near a Hemlock

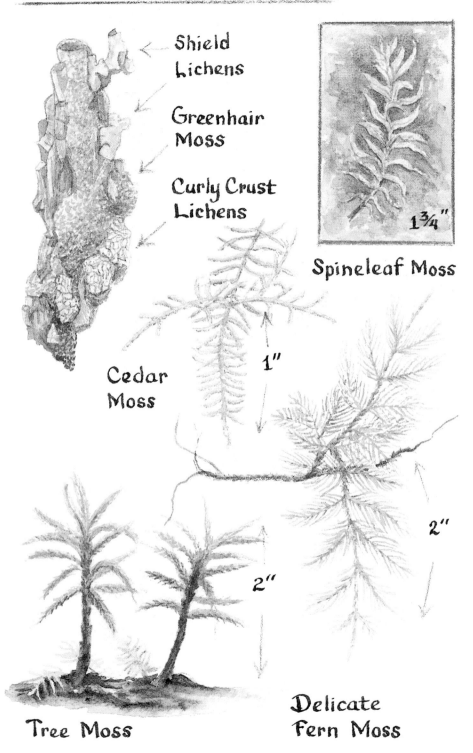

Shield Lichens

Greenhair Moss

Curly Crust Lichens

Spineleaf Moss

1¾"

Cedar Moss

1"

Tree Moss

2"

2"

Delicate Fern Moss

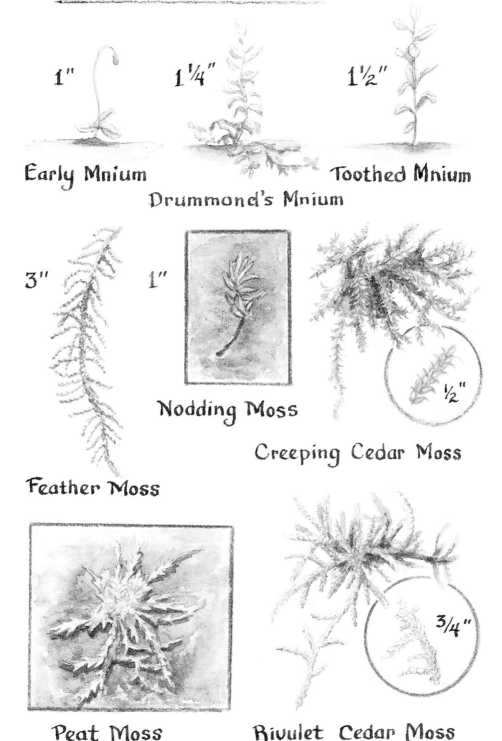

1"

Early Mnium

1¼"

Drummond's Mnium

1½"

Toothed Mnium

3"

Feather Moss

1"

Nodding Moss

½"

Creeping Cedar Moss

Peat Moss

¾"

Rivulet Cedar Moss

April 30 ~
  Where the stream takes
a sharp bend to the east,
the ground is low and boggy.
Peat Moss rises in spongy
clumps here and there.

  False Hellebore, or Indian Poke,
growing in abundance in all the wet
places, is now 18-24" high. Green
flowers appear in June; then the
plant withers.

  Fertile fronds of
Sensitive Ferns sprout
up close to the stream.
In the summer, these
ferns are home base
for dozens of black
damselflies glowing
blue or green in the
sunlight.

  Dwarfed by an
Indian Poke are two
little Sessile-leaved
Bellworts, or Wild Oats,
shyly bending their
delicate white flowers.

Half a mile up from the stream, among the maples and red spruces, birches and aspens of the "Upper Woods," Interrupted Fern fiddle-heads line the path.

At the eastern end of the path are Kidneyleaf Buttercups, small plants with inconspicuous yellow flowers.

An Elderberry bush, protected by the old colonial stone wall, is almost ready to bloom.

30° snow flurries. 6 Deer headed up north meadow around noon. Downy Woodpecker at suet feeder.

50° sunny. Discovered dead Deer impaled on sharp branch of log in stream.

Foggy. 24 Robins on lawn; Grackles and Cowbirds at feeders; Ducks on pond.

Rain PM. Woodchuck in north meadow.

40° overcast and windy. Ferns and plants near stream showing signs of green. Only signs of activity near pond and stream: songs of Chickadees and Song Sparrows; and a Great Blue Heron flying downstream.

28°, 7 AM, snow flurries PM. Pine Siskins fed on Aspen catkins. At pond: 2 Ducks and a Belted Kingfisher. Large Aspen and fallen Beech trees are being gnawed by a Beaver. Heard Wild Turkeys in the woods.

34-40° snow flurries. Set out 4 Bluebird boxes that Bernie constructed.

Daffodils had caps of snow. Goldfinches at thistle feeder; Cardinals at A-frame.

28° 7 AM. At the feeders: Pine Siskins, Purple and House Finches, Goldfinches, Nuthatches, Song Sparrows, Chickadees, Cardinals, Doves, Juncos, Cowbirds and Blue Jays.

60's, sunny. Spring Peepers are in full chorus. Heard Phoebes and Wild Turkeys. Deer carcass in stream half consumed.

19 — 40° 7 AM, cloudy. B. found a dead Golden-crowned Kinglet behind Spruce on lawn. We watched Beaver paddle around pond PM.

21 — Cloudy, drizzly. A Red-breasted Nuthatch has been coming to feeders lately.

22 — Snowed all day and night — 6-8"!

23 — Snow flurries until afternoon. All birds busy at feeders. New addition: a female Red-winged Blackbird. Only the Grackles could get her out of the A-frame. White-throated and Chipping Sparrows forage in the woods.

25 — 70° afternoon. Only a few patches of snow are left. Water flowing swiftly in stream.

26 — 65° sunny. Chipping and White-throated Sparrows at feeders; also Chipmunk and Rabbit underneath. At pond: watched Beaver through binoculars until he sensed me, slapped his tail, and dove under water.

27 — Pond visit early afternoon: didn't see Beaver, but one of the Gray Birches is down.

28 — 8 AM: You could hear Red-winged Blackbirds staking claims all over the place. Found a place to observe Beaver for ½ hour without spooking him.

29 — Downy Woodpecker in Scotch Pines. Bumblebees on Blue Ajuga.

30 — Foggy, 8:50 AM: A flock of Canadian Geese lost their bearings. They flew low, honking loudly. They headed S, then W, finally N.

MAY

Fritillary
Northern
White Violets

Sensitive Fern
Marsh Blue Violets

Swallowtail   Woodfern
Foam Flowers   Swamp Buttercups

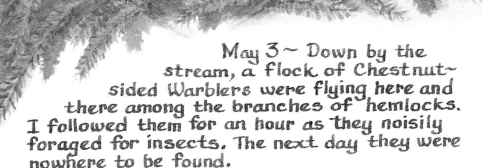

May 3 ~ Down by the stream, a flock of Chestnut-sided Warblers were flying here and there among the branches of hemlocks. I followed them for an hour as they noisily foraged for insects. The next day they were nowhere to be found.

These migrating birds raise only one brood each spring; and are frequently victimized when cowbirds leave their eggs for these warblers to incubate.

They breed from southern Canada to east-central U.S., and winter in Central America.

May 6 ~ This Eastern Towhee was under the feeders early this morning, busily hopping backwards, scratching up seeds and insects, typical behavior for this bird.

Formerly known as the Rufous-sided Towhee, it has red eyes. Towhees in the southeast have white eyes. Northern Towhees go south for the winter where they are seen together. They also are unwitting victims of cowbirds.

May 15~
    While searching for
Wood Thrushes heard in the white
pines north of the house, I saw a flash of
yellow, black and white flitting from branch
to branch in the undergrowth. A Magnolia
Warbler settled on a branch just long enough
for me to snap a photo.

    It breeds in the north, but was discovered
among magnolias in the south in 1810, therefore
its name. It winters from Mexico to Central
America.

May 6~
    Two White-crowned Sparrows were eat-
ing fallen seeds on the ground, spilled by
many birds at the feeders. I counted
9 Blue Jays, 2 Cardinals, 2 Nuthatches,
24 Goldfinches, 12 Purple Finches, and
numerous Doves, Juncos and Chickadees.

    White-crowned Sparrows nest in the far
north and mountains of the west. They
            winter in the U.S., Mexico and Cuba.

← May 1 ~ Purple Trilliums, also known as Wetdog Trilliums and Stinking Benjamins due to their bad odor, appeared among the rocks and boulders under the maples.

Early herbalists used this plant to treat gangrene.   8-16"

→ May 3 ~ Wood Anemones, found in the meadow near the hemlocks, last only two weeks. The flowers close at night.   4-8"

← May 15 ~ Goldthreads get their name from the golden-yellow under-ground stem which was chewed by both Indians and colonists to treat mouth sores. Another name was Canker-root. Also used as an eyewash and a yellow dye.   3-6"

→

May 15 ~ Painted
Trilliums came into
bloom two weeks
after the Purple
    Trilliums at a
    far-removed
    location - where
the hemlocks border
the south meadow.
                8-20"

←

May 17 ~ Starflowers
grow among Mayflowers
and Goldthreads in the
spongy, acid soil beneath
the hemlocks near the
stream.   4-8"

May 18 ~ Canada May-
flowers, found near
the stream, spread by
rhizomes and form
colonies. Unusual for
a member of the
    Lily Family, each
    flower has only
    2 petals, 2 sepals,
and 4 stamens in-
stead of the typical
3-3-6 pattern. Also
called Wild Lily-of-
the-Valley.   2-6"

A Chipmunk lives under the back porch steps, conveniently near the bird feeders. They're labelled ground-dwelling squirrels, but are capable of climbing when the rewards are great, as seen above.

Chipmunks are omnivorous. Besides their passion for storing seeds and nuts, they eat vegetables, fruits, insects, worms, snails, eggs, frogs, and even small snakes and birds.

They aren't true hibernators, but do go underground into chambered burrows in autumn, and don't usually emerge until spring. They don't rely on body fat, but on stored food. That's why we see them stuffing their cheek pouches with as many as 70 sunflower seeds to deposit underground.

The underground burrow can extend 30 feet or more with tunnels leading to rooms for sleeping, storage and latrine. Chipmunks plug their entrances when they go underground. They wake every so often to eat the stored food.

8-10"

3 oz.

Eastern
Chipmunk

Woodchucks, also called Groundhogs, are celebrated for supposedly helping to predict the length of winter. According to legend, on Groundhog Day, February 2, if the Groundhog emerges from his den and sees his shadow, 6 more weeks of winter will follow.

The snow is too deep here in February for them to emerge and be seen, or for us to emerge to see them. The earliest we've seen one was in March. I did a doubletake the first of May when spotting a Woodchuck sitting on top a fencepost by the road. The one shown above was ambling across the lawn headed for the garden.

Woodchucks are true hibernators. Unlike the Chipmunk who stores food underground, the Woodchuck relies on its own body fat to survive the winter in a comalike state.

They dig burrows up to 30 feet with side tunnels leading to rooms for hibernating, raising young, and for waste disposal, plus one or two back holes for escape routes.

Woodchuck   2'   5-15 lbs.

A Great Blue Heron comes to the pond often starting in May, but usually we catch sight of it flying over the stream, its great wings spanning seven feet, flapping slowly.

It stands four feet tall and walks stiffly on long stilt legs.

Its main food is fish, amphibians and crustaceans, but it also eats insects, rodents and birds. It jabs its prey with its bill.

Generally quiet, the Great Blue Heron will give deep, harsh croaks when disturbed.

May 7~

This Green Heron was walking away from the pond with its neck extended before it flew into the woods.

May 8 — This is the same bird in two other poses by the pond.

The Green Heron is very vocal, its normal call a sharp "skow."

Also called the Green-backed Heron, it stands 16-22" tall, and feeds on fish, salamanders, frogs, and small land animals.

VIOLETS

First of the violets
to appear, stretching
blue faces above dead
leaves and twigs on
the old colonial path
above the road are
Common Blue Violets.
3-8"

Shortly thereafter
Dog Violets spring up
throughout the fields.
Leaves and flowers
grow on the same
stalk.   2-6"

The only yellow
violets found so far
are Round-leaved
Yellow Violets grow-
ing on a bank by the
stream.   2-5"

Sweet White Violets
bloom beneath the
canopies of the
spruces, pines and
hemlocks.   3-5"

Northern White Violets
favor wetter grounds
along the stream and
pond runoff.   1-5"

The last and
largest are
Marsh Blue
Violets that
share a wet,
shady habitat
by the pond
runoff with
Northern White
Violets, Swamp
Buttercups,
Foamflowers,
and various
ferns.   5-10"

May 6 ~

A sharp
metallic "clink"
drew me to the
window where I saw
a male Rose-breasted
Grosbeak watching the
commotion at the feeders.
He returned a few days later
to eat during a heavy rainfall.

May 13 ~ On another rainy day, two
female Grosbeaks filled up
at one of
the feeders
before
leaving
for their
breeding
area.

May 9 ~

A female Northern Oriole tried to reach the sugar water in the hummingbird feeder from its perch on a hydrangea branch. She couldn't get close enough, and flew away after several attempts.

May 9 ~

The hydrangea held an added delight that same morning. An Indigo Bunting watched the activity at the feeders; but he stayed only long enough for me to photograph his iridescent beauty in the sunlight.

Only the males are blue. The females are brown with faintly streaked underparts.

10"
Bird's-eye
Speedwell

Dwarf Ginseng 6"

18" Mayapple; Mandrake

Smaller Pussytoes 6"

Yellow
Clintonia;
Bluebead
Lily   8"

2'
Jack-in-the-Pulpit

Winter Cress   2'
Barren Strawberry   6"

MAY—

1 ~ 60°. Spotted a Woodchuck sitting upright on a fencepost near the barn.

3 ~ At feeders: male Cardinal feeds female on porch of mailbox feeder; Cowbird eats inside mailbox; Chipping Sparrows at teahouse; Goldfinches at niger seed feeder; Doves and Blue Jays eat on ground beneath feeders. Watched Chestnut-sided Warblers at stream.

6 ~ 80° by 10:30. Rufous-sided Towhee and White-crowned Sparrows under feeders AM; male Rose-breasted Grosbeak PM. Oddity: a Blue Jay was using its body to make the teahouse feeder sway back and forth in time to music coming through an open window.

7 ~ 70°. Green Heron at pond. Cottontail Rabbits and Woodchucks in yard and meadow.

9 ~ 60's, sunny. Serviceberry and Quince trees blooming. 24 Pine Siskins at feeders AM; male Indigo Bunting and female Baltimore Oriole later.

10 ~ Heavy rain. Male Rose-breasted Grosbeak returned. Nests beginning in Bluebird houses.

12 ~ Cloudy, some rain. Male Baltimore Oriole in Maple near barn.

13 ~ More rain. Male Rose-breasted Grosbeak returned plus 2 female Grosbeaks. A male House Wren uses the back porch railing to loudly warble his territorial claim.

14 ~ A female Phoebe is rebuilding the nest they always use under the 2nd story eaves. Red-winged Blackbirds visited feeders.

15 ~ Sunny and warm. Heard Brown Thrasher in backyard Spruces and Wood Thrushes in the White Pines. Found a Magnolia Warbler in the White Pine woods.

16 ~ 80°. Goldfinches are all over backyard eating Dandelion seeds. Black Cherry trees now blooming.

17 ~ AM: Watched the Great Blue Heron fly over stream. Followed a Yellow-shafted Flicker as it walked and pecked its way around the pond. PM: Watched the Beaver chew wood in the pond.

20 ~ 85°, hot and humid. Barn Swallows perform aerial stunts chasing insects near barn. Trees are half leafed out. Pond is full of seeds and catkins from Birch, Beech, Aspen and Maple trees.

22 ~ Chokecherry and Apple trees now in bloom. Bluebird Houses: N. field ~ 2 pink eggs; near pond ~ 7 tiny eggs; S. path ~ empty; near garden ~ no eggs yet.

25 ~ 80°. Saw 4 Swallowtail Butterflies feeding on dung. Copper and Skipper Butterflies everywhere. Damselflies hover over pond. Found Horsetails growing on W. side of pond.

29 ~ 75°. Pond is brown and scummy with tree detritus. A Red Squirrel grabbed a Brown-headed Cowbird in the mailbox feeder and threw it out!

31 ~ 90° humid, thundershowers PM. House Wrens are building trial nests everywhere ~ inside tool shed, under porch sidings, in a Bluebird house, even the bird feeders.

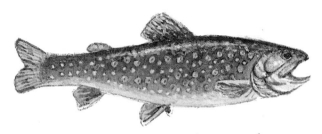

The salamanders
we see swimming
in the pond are Eastern
Newts. They go through
two adult phases. The
orange-red newts, called efts,
live on land for 2-3 years. They then
change color and return to water to
breed. The eggs hatch and the larvae develop
in water until late summer when they lose
their gills, grow legs and walk away.

Brook Trout, found and caught in our
stream, are devoured by two-legged
unrepentant predators.

The frogs around the pond usually plop
into the water before we can see them.
This Bullfrog, however, surprised us by
posing for closeups. Bullfrog tadpoles
spend 2-3 years
in water before
exchanging gills
and fins for lungs
and legs. They
stay close to the
water's edge as
adults.

June 5 ~ We were more astonished to see
this gray fox come out of our fenced-in
blueberry patch at high noon. Maybe he was
the culprit who broke the door. He returned
the next day to snoop around inside the fence,
possibly checking to see if the berries were ripe.

They usually hunt at night for small mammals,
insects, lizards, and birds, and also eat nuts,
fruits and berries. The gray fox is the only
member of the dog family that climbs trees!

Length: 31-44"   Weight: 8-10 lbs.

In the

Field Hawkweed

Orange Hawkweed

Mouse-ear Hawkweed

Daisy Fleabane

Rough-fruited Cinquefoil

Mourning Cloak

Blue-eyed Grass

Meadow

Tall Buttercup
  Yarrow Wild Madder
Common Cinquefoil   Goatsbeard
            Wild Strawberry

June 4, 8 A.M. —

We took pictures of a doe wandering around our backyard as if in search of something, possibly a place to give birth.

Most fawns are born the last of May and early June. A doe can produce a fawn at age one. After the first year twin offspring are most common. Does can breed for fifteen years if they live that long. Four to five years is the average life-span.

The breeding period, or rutting season, lasts from late October to late November. The gestation period is about 205 days.

Fawns born each year increase the herd size 20-30%.

A favorite place for does to hide their fawns is the middle of a meadow. The fawns, weighing 4-5 pounds at birth, will remain concealed in high grass until able to follow their mother around. Their spotted coats blend into almost any background.

June 10 — We observed a doe out in the meadow suckling one of her offspring. The doe's udder has four nipples, so she could nurse four fawns at the same time. She will return 8-10 times during a 24-hour period to feed her young, but doesn't stay with them lest her body scent betray their presence to predators. For the first 3 or 4 days fawns are odorless.

June 15 — Barn Swallows keep Bernie
company when he mows the fields. They
swoop in and around him, snapping up
insects stirred up by the tractor. At dusk
we watch their swift acrobatics as they
catch mosquitoes. More power to them!

They make mud and straw nests in barn
lofts (if they can get in), or under overhanging eaves. An average of 5 white
eggs, spotted with brown, are laid.

The male and female take turns incubating the eggs for 15 days. Nestlings are fed live insects by both parents. After 18-20 days, father will train them to forage while mother lays another set of eggs.

At the end of summer swallows flock together on telephone lines, then gather along the coast to feed and roost before migrating to Central and South America.

Musk Mallow 2'
Cow Vetch 2'
Red Clover 8"
Birdfoot Trefoil 1'

By the Stream

2' Ragged Robin
2' Golden Ragwort
18" Seedbox
8" Forget-me-not

DRAGONFLIES

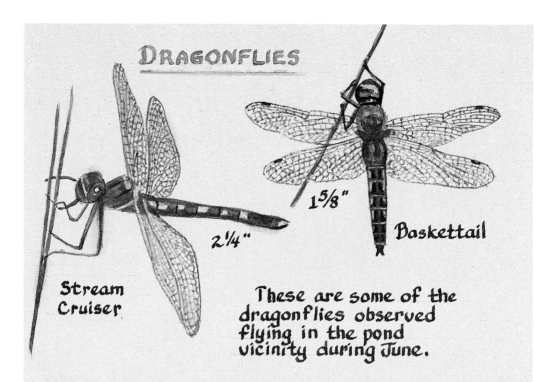

2¼"

1⅝"

Baskettail

Stream Cruiser

These are some of the dragonflies observed flying in the pond vicinity during June.

We see dragonflies darting about the pond, stream and wetlands only when it's sunny. Some have favorite perches; some are very aggressive about their territories, and then we witness aerial combat.

They can fly forwards, backwards, sideways, up and down, or stop abruptly and hover. It's extremely difficult to either catch them or to photograph them.

Some can fly up to 35 mph!

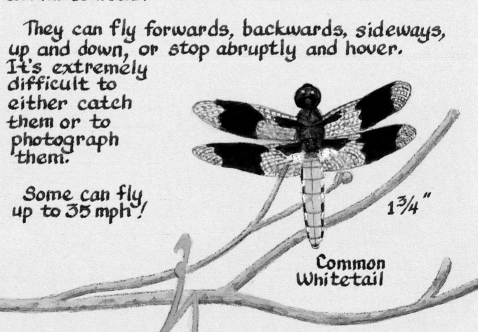

1¾"

Common Whitetail

DAMSELFLIES

Bluet
(Narrow-winged)
1¼"

Slender Bluets hover and roam amid the vegetation lining the shores of the pond and stream.

Ebony Jewelwing
(Broad-winged)

1⅞"

Ebony Jewelwings patrol the stream in large numbers, the bodies of the males gleaming metallic blue or green.

Damselflies fold their wings together when resting. Dragonflies rest with their wings outspread.

Both insects are beneficial for eating large quantities of mosquitoes as well as other flying insects. They lay eggs on or in water and in plant tissue. The nymphs that hatch spend one or more years under water, molting many times before ready to emerge. Then they climb up a plant stem, crawl out of their case, dry off and fly to woods or fields. When they mature in 2-3 weeks, they return to stream or pond.

A~
Chicory
3'

B~
Willow
Herb
2'

C~
Wild
Basil
8"

A~
Deptford
Pink
20"

B~
Maiden
Pink
10"

C~
Blue
Vervain
4'

A B C

June 26 — A pair of Common Yellowthroats
nervously hopped in a Scotch Pine and started
making "chipping" sounds when I approached
the tree. We also see them in thickets next
to the meadows and in the hemlocks by the
stream.

Like other wood warblers they're elusive,
and their quick movements in search of insects
make photographing them difficult.

The young leave the nest before they can fly,
and are fed on the ground. The fledgling
phase lasts 2-3 weeks, longer than that of
most other warblers.

Warblers are nocturnal migrants. Large
numbers of Yellowthroats lose their lives in
storms, foggy weather, and from flying into tall
buildings and lighthouses during migration.

Fuschias and a feeder brought Ruby-throated Hummingbirds to our terrace this summer. We added another feeder around the corner to reduce the fighting, but it only increased the number of hummingbirds and their aerial battles.

Our greatest delight is when one of the birds notices us sitting there. It darts in front of each of us, hovers, and emits a tiny squeak before checking out the next.

It is the smallest North American bird—3-3½"; it can hover and fly backwards; its wings vibrate up to 75 beats per second. For all the energy it expends defending its territory it has to refuel 50-60 times a day, sucking up nectar and insects through a tubular tongue. To stretch its energy reserves at night, it can go into a state of torpor, dropping its temperature and energy output.

The Rubythroat is the only hummingbird that nests east of the Mississippi. It travels as much as 2,000 miles to its winter range.

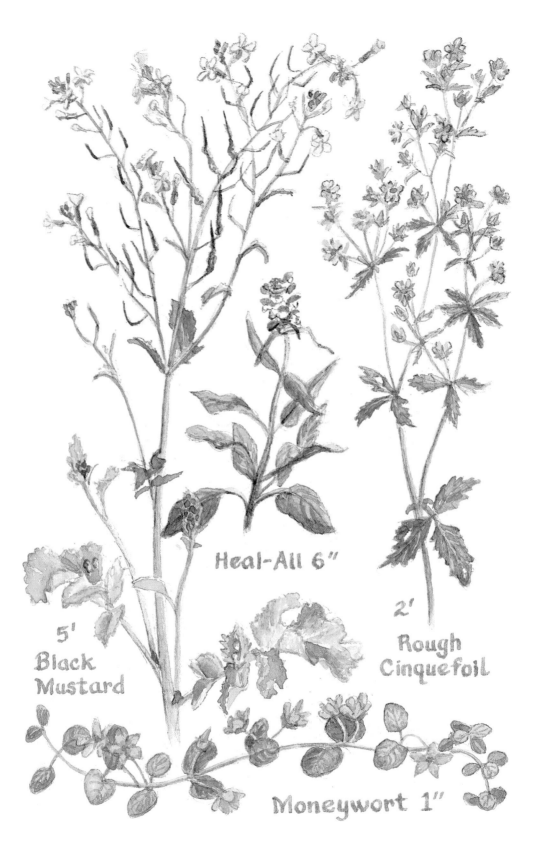

Heal-All 6"

5'
Black
Mustard

2'
Rough
Cinquefoil

Moneywort 1"

2'
Pale Smartweed

Sundrops 8"

3'
Yellow Avens

Partridgeberry 1"

1. Napkin Amanita
2. Caesar's Mushroom
3. Birch Bolete
4. Blackish-red Russula
5. Scaly Vase
   Chanterelle
6. Brown Velvet
   Lactarius

1. Coker's Amanita   2. Yellow-orange Fly Agaric
3. Destroying Angel   4. Dye Polyphore
5. Doughnut Fungus   6. Pungent Russula
        7. Almond-scented Russula

JUNE ~

2 ~ Clear, pleasant, breezy. At pond: Dragonflies, Damselflies, Salamanders, Frogs. Scarlet Tanager in Hemlocks. Mourning Cloak Butterfly in front yard.

3 ~ 70° sunny, breezy. Watched Phoebe swoop up and down from clothesline to catch insects. Caught a glimpse of a male Yellowthroat in middle thicket.

4 ~ 8 AM: A Doe wandered around backyard and S. meadow as if searching for something. Barn Swallows are back.

5 ~ High 60's, sunny. B. saw a Gray Fox behind the barn. I searched the whole property for it. Finally saw it coming from blueberries.

6 ~ 4 PM: The Gray Fox roamed all over the yard, then loped through the woods.

9 ~ 50's, partly cloudy. Rained the last 2 days. Cedar Waxwings are back.

10 ~ The Doe must have been looking for a place to give birth. She was in the S. meadow nursing a Fawn. House Finches flock to the thistle feeder. Pond is swarming with Dragonflies, Damselflies and Butterflies.

11 ~ Wildflowers are blooming everywhere: in the meadow, woods, and around the pond.

12 ~ New bird at feeders – a Red Crossbill. Regular clients: Purple and House Finches, Grackles, House Sparrows, Cowbirds, Nuthatches, Blue Jays, Cardinals and an occasional Redwinged Blackbird. We hear Song Sparrows, Phoebes, Vireos and House Wrens.

13 ~ B. saw the Doe and baby Fawn run down the S. meadow. Later he found a dead Downy Woodpecker nestling near the house.

15 ~ Beautiful sunny, dry weather. Barn Swallows circled Bernie as he mowed the fields and they scooped up insects.

16 ~ 70's, pleasant. The word is out... 3 dozen Barn Swallows showed up to feast on the insects kicked up by B's tractor-mower.

22 ~ 60's. Rained during night. A Raccoon darted up a tree and kept itself hidden when I showed up in the White Pine woods.

23 ~ Watched a Cedar Waxwing building a nest in one of the Blue Spruce trees.

26 ~ At pond: a Turtle was floating in the middle; Frogs were sunning themselves along the banks. Near barn: Yellowthroats hopped around in the Scotch Pines.

27 ~ 8:30 AM at pond: Dragonflies not airborne yet; Bullfrog rumbling. There are baby chick-adees in lowest "bluebird" birdhouse. Those in house near garden met an ill fate. Finch fledglings are begging near feeders. Robin young are cheeping after parents on lawn. Tiger Swallowtails are everywhere.

28 ~ 36° at 6:30 AM; 80° at 3:00 PM. 6 Ruffed Grouse took flight right in front of me on the path down to the N. meadow.

30 ~ 65-70° partly sunny. Male Cardinal feeding fledgling in bushes near feeders. Copper, Skipper, Fritillary Butterflies abundant.

JULY

← ———— July 10 ~ Twin fawns came to the edge of a grassy glade to watch me picking raspberries. Their mother had to be far afield or she would have snorted and had them out of there within a few seconds of my appearance.

Taking advantage of her absence, I crooned to them and edged closer; but they bolted after a few minutes of my singing.

Later in the week, I surprised them as they were drinking at the stream. This time their departure was swift and certain, and they bounded into the hemlock woods.

July 15 ~ The best experience I've had photographing deer happened this evening. I crept up to an ironwood clump within camera range of two deer, without their hearing, seeing or smelling me. The click of the camera alerted them, however. They gingerly approached the source of the sound, then leaped away as I snapped more pictures. But their curiosity got the better of them and they kept returning and leaping away until I ran out of film and showed myself. ———→

By the Stream

A. Turtlehead 2'
B. Bittersweet Nightshade 3'
C. Square-stemmed Monkey Flower 3'
D. Bee Balm; Oswego Tea 3'

A.
Swamp Candle;
Yellow Loosestrife 18"

B.

C.

D.
Fringed
Loosestrife
2'

B. Cardinal Flower 2'

C. Spotted Touch-me-not; Jewelweed 18"

1. Twelve-spotted Skimmer   2. Female Whitetail
3. Four-spotted Skimmer
4. Chalk-fronted Corporal   5. Immature Widow

There are about 450 species of dragonflies and damselflies in North America. Fossils show they existed 300 million years ago.

They spend more of their lives underwater as nymphs than above. There they consume insect larvae, tadpoles and even small fish. As adults, they catch and eat flying insects.

6. Widow Skimmer

7. Yellow-legged
   Meadowhawk

8. Cherry-faced
   Meadowhawks

9. Ebony Jewelwing Damselflies

Both damselflies and dragonflies mate in a "wheel" position in flight or at rest. The male transfers sperm to his 2nd abdominal segment and the female extends the tip of her abdomen to receive it. Generally, the male keeps his hold on her until she has laid her eggs in water.

Monarch
3½ – 4"

Eastern
Tiger
Swallowtail

4 – 5⅞"

A Monarch and Tiger Swallowtail were drinking nectar from this milkweed at the same time, changing positions without any hostility.

The Monarch is one of the Milkweed Butterflies whose caterpillars feed on milkweeds and other poisonous plants. It is the only butterfly that migrates north and south. Eastern and midwestern Monarchs fly all the way to Mexico for winter. In the west they overwinter in pine, cypress and eucalyptus groves in California.

The Eastern Tiger Swallowtail is one of the most common butterflies east of the Rocky Mountains, abounding in wooded forests of the Appalachian Range. They hibernate in chrysalis form.

Several Red-spotted Purples visited the blueberries daily, and occasionally a White Admiral fluttered in.

The White Admiral ranges from coast to coast in Canada and the northern states from Minnesota to Maine.

The Red-spotted Purple can be found in most of the U.S. Along the northern edge of its range it hybridizes with the White Admiral, producing partially banded offspring.

The undersides of both are similar except for the white bands of the White Admiral.

They both hibernate as caterpillars, rolled up in leaves tied to the stem with silk.

White Admiral

2⅞ – 3⅛ "

Red-spotted Purple

3 – 3⅜ "

30"
Bladder
Campion

20"
Rough
Avens

Mayweed 8"

Wild Leek 12"

3'
White
Sweet
Clover

Tall
Meadow
Rue 3'

Smaller Enchanter's
Nightshade 5"

Foxgloves 2'

Cedar Waxwings, traveling in flocks, visit almost every state at any time of year. We can depend on them coming here shortly before our blueberries ripen, and we listen for their high-pitched "seee" from the pines.

The red waxlike tips on the secondary feathers and their fondness for cedar berries give them their common name.

Sometimes a group of Cedar Waxwings will line up on a limb and pass a berry from beak to beak until one of them eats it. They nest late in the summer when there is an ample supply of berries to feed the nestlings.

They are known to become inebriated after eating overripe fruit.

When they're not eating our berries, they're down by the stream catching insects.

Catbirds love blue-berries, and scold us when we're picking them. Their dull color is compensated for by their entertaining mimi-cry of other birds. Cat-like calls give them their name.

Several Eastern Kingbirds sampled our blue-berries for a few days, then vanished. Their primary food is insects.

The Latin name of these fly-catchers, "Tyrannus tyrannus," expresses their very aggressive behavior which ex-tends to attacking crows, owls, vultures and hawks. Flying at their victims from above, they strike at their backs, pulling out feathers.

Afterwards, they may fly up high, then descend doing a series of short glides and acrobatic tumbles.

4'
Mullein

2'
Butter-and-eggs

3'
St. Johnswort

6"
Yellow Sorrel

4'
Evening Primrose
18"
Black-eyed Susan
2'
Yellow Cress
6"
Hop Clover

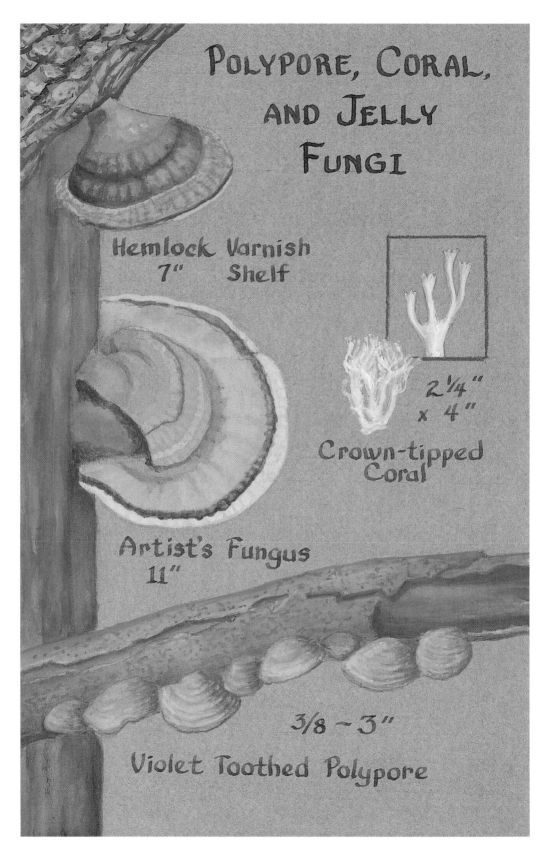

POLYPORE, CORAL, AND JELLY FUNGI

Hemlock Varnish Shelf
7"

Crown-tipped Coral
2 1/4" x 4"

Artist's Fungus
11"

Violet Toothed Polypore
3/8 ~ 3"

Witches'
Butter
3/4 ~ 4"

5"
x 7"

Hoof
Fungus
7"

Yellow-tipped Coral

Multicolored Gill Polypore
1 ~ 4"

1/4 ~ 3/8"

Silky Parchment

July 22 —

I watched a Robin scolding and chasing a
Belted Kingfisher across the pond and around
and around until the Kingfisher gave up and
left. The ruckus brought a pair of Scarlet
Tanagers on the scene, apparently to see
what all the fuss was about.

I can imagine what happened. The Belted
Kingfisher's favorite perch for spying and
catching fish in the pond is very close to
where the Robins have set up a nest. I am
always "attacked" whenever I walk on that
side of the pond. One of the Robins flies
straight toward my head, then veers off
at the last second.

The nest is on a low branch, overhanging
the path around the pond, and easily
visible from beneath. They will raise
2-3 broods a year.

We've been scolded by the Kingfisher, too, when we have dared to fish in his domain. We hear his "rat-a-tat-tat" call as he patrols the stream. Before eating a fish he cracks its head against a branch. If it's large he goes into contortions swallowing it.

The Scarlet Tanagers stay deep in the woods, eating insects, caterpillars and some berries. This is only the third time I've seen them this summer. The winter plumage of the male changes from scarlet and black to dull green and brown.

Tanagers and Kingfishers raise only one brood each year.

I found this Pearl Crescent resting among clover in the meadow. They fly low over the grasses, and can be found on puddles and flowers. Adults go for the nectar in composite flowers. Eggs are laid in clusters on aster leaves and they all chew en masse when they hatch.

When I came along, this handsome Orb Weaver was wrapping up a victim she had caught in her web by the pond. When these spiders feel a vibration in the web strands, they rush to the insect, bite it, wrap it in silk, then suck out the body fluids, or save it to eat later.

Something strange on a buttercup drew me closer and I saw a crablike creature. It's called a Red-spotted Crab Spider. It can be found on white or yellow flowers and can change color to blend with the petals. Here it waits to ambush flower-visiting insects.

Many of the butterflies in the pond vicinity are Meadow Fritillaries. They are among the most abundant bog fritillary butterflies in the East. Composite flowers are their favorite nectar source. Caterpillars feed on violet leaves.

Every summer a Black and Yellow Argiope weaves a circular web at the edge of the white pines. The female hangs head down in the center, ready to wrap up any flying insect caught in the sticky web. The male is smaller and builds a smaller web.

On the way up to the south meadow, I took a photo of a Virginia Ctenuchid Moth on a yarrow flower. All Ctenuchids visit flowers and fly during the day.

Most moths fly at night, and so we're not aware of them. However, there are many more species of moths than of butterflies.

Hedge Bindweed
6'

18"

Lesser
Stitchwort

White Clover   5"   Indian Pipes 10"

Queen Anne's
Lace

3'

18"

Rough
Bedstraw

Shinleaf 10"

Wood Sorrel 4"

118

July —

3 — 80°, sunny. 2 Bobolinks in the meadow kept flying around me, chirping wildly. I must have come too close to their nest.

4 — 80°, hazy, humid. A Yellow-rumped Warbler fluttered outside the living room window. Watched a Doe nurse her Fawn in north meadow. Rained all night.

5 — Drizzly. Yellow-rumped Warbler now flying at back porch window. 2 Cedar Waxwings on front porch eating paint flakes we scraped off prior to painting.

7 — Ruby-throated Hummingbirds fighting over fuschias.

8 — B. saw Gray Fox down in S. meadow. Evening Grosbeaks at feeders.

9 — Hot and humid. A Song Sparrow followed me as I passed the middle woods. 8 PM: Gray Fox seen near garden.

10 — High 80's, humid. Twin Fawns watched me as I picked raspberries. Belted Kingfisher scolded Deer that walked around pond.

12 — Cloudy. Yellow-rumped Warbler now flying at barn windows.

15 — 70°. Came upon twin Fawns at stream; also many Cedar Waxwings and the Blue Heron. 7 PM: Photo session with 2 inquisitive but suspicious does in meadow.

17 — A Blackpoll Warbler came to the niger seed feeder.

18 — 75°, humid. A flock of 12-16 Cedar Waxwings flitted around grasses and weeds near pond. Yellowthroats across road were upset when I came by. More nests, probably.

19 — Several Goldfinches bathed in stream. The Blue Heron flew away as usual. Ebony Jewel-wing Damselflies are mating.

22 — 75°. At pond: This time a Robin chased away the Belted Kingfisher. Scarlet Tanagers came out of the woods to watch.

23 — Turkey Vultures at work on Deer killed on road.

25 — 80°, humid. Eastern Kingbirds joined the Cedar Waxwings, Catbirds, Cardinals, Robins, War-blers, Red-spotted Purple and White Admiral Butterflies feed on our blueberries.

27 — Hundreds of Orb Weaver Spiders' webs built between tall meadow grasses. Green Darner Dragonfly swooped all around pond.

28 — Foggy AM, 85° PM. Red Admiral Butterfly at pond. Huge Snapping Turtle, on rocks near water, slipped into water before I could raise camera. Male Cardinal brought 2 fledglings to Spruce tree near feeders.

29 — Afternoon thunderstorm with ½" hail.

30 — Stream is full and swift after yesterday's heavy rain. Many mushrooms and Indian Pipes. Still lots of Raspberries. Black-berries beginning to ripen.

31 — More heavy rain.

AUGUST

POND

Water
Hemlock
3'

3'

Water
Plantain

1½'

Bur
Marigold

Grass-leaved
Arrowhead 1½'

FLOWERS

Pale
Smartweed
6'

Swamp
Beggar
Ticks 5'

3½'
Broad-leaved
Arrowhead

2'
Bottle
Gentian

Northern Pearly Eye

Bluebottle
Fly

Short-winged
Blister Beetle

Skipper on
Blue Vervain

Swallowtail
Larva on
Early Goldenrod

Five-banded
Tiphiid Wasp

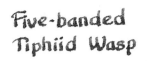

Sulphur on Buttercup

Black Pine Sawyer

Great-Spangled ↑
Fritillary on
Orange Hawkweed

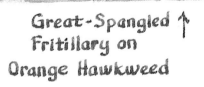

Cabbage Butterfly
on Tufted Vetch ⟶

August 15 —

Today I made another attempt to photograph the Great Blue Heron who hangs out by the pond. I carried nothing but a camera equipped with a 500 mm. lens so I could focus if it took flight.

I stealthily crept down to the pond, but there was no sign of the heron.

As I wandered past the pond, I startled a buck who had been sleeping in the ferns. He didn't bolt as deer generally do.

Even though he was too close for the 500 mm. lens, I used up all the film meant for the heron as he stood there and stared at me.

I was eager to put more film into the camera, change the lens and gather the rest of my gear. Quickly I made my way back around the pond and up the hill.

Incredibly...the buck followed me.

But he stopped at the foot of the path leading up the hill.

Now equipped with a new roll of film and a smaller mm. zoom lens, I came downhill with expectations of getting great photos of this unusually friendly deer.

He was nowhere in sight.

But the Great Blue Heron was!

It rose majestically and flapped away.

Another great opportunity, and I had the wrong lens on the camera...again.

I searched everywhere for the buck, and finally spotted him browsing across the stream.

Because of the distance, I switched to the 500 mm. lens. At last! The right lighting, the right lens!

But then he looked in my direction and headed straight for me. He came so close I had to change the lens again!

My actions with the camera startled him. He stopped, turned, then loped around the pond and up to the fields.

On my way uphill through the north meadow, I saw the buck resting under larch trees.

I loitered, and found wildflowers to photograph on the other side of the larches.

Sure enough, his curiosity prevailed. He walked around the trees to investigate.

This time I was prepared for a close encounter, and was able to get four good photos before he listened to his inner voice.

He retreated towards the woods, but stopped to watch as I picked up my gear and went up the hill.

Strange behavior for a Whitetailed Deer in prime hunting territory!

3-6'

Tall
Goldenrod

2-4'

Lance-
leaved
Goldenrod

1-7'

Rough-stemmed
Goldenrod

Showy
Goldenrod
2-6'

Late
Goldenrod

2-5'

Bog
Goldenrod

2-7'

Viceroy

2⅝ ~ 3″ wingspan

2 broods

Red Admiral

1¾ ~ 2¼″ wingspan

2 broods

The Viceroy looks and acts like a Monarch butterfly, but it is smaller, with curved black lines crossing the hindwings. The similarity saves it from predators who don't like the taste of Monarchs.

Unlike the Monarchs who migrate, the Viceroys overwinter as larvae in rolled leaves attached to twigs.

Red Admirals are found worldwide in temperate regions wherever hops and nettles grow. Those we see come from the south each spring. That may account for the bedraggled appearance of the one shown above.

Males are territorial and will dart at other butterflies, moths, even people.

The erratic flight of Wood Nymphs in and out of the woods makes them most difficult to photograph. The one below did light for a moment on meadowsweet; but they favor tree sap, rotting fruit, fungi and animal remains.

The caterpillars hibernate before feeding, emerging from chrysalides in late summer.

The Question Mark butterfly, named for the swirl and dot on the underside of each hindwing, is also called Violet-tip for the color edging its wings. The adults love sap and rotting fruit, and sometimes get tipsy when fruit ferments.

They hibernate in butterfly form in dark, sheltered places.

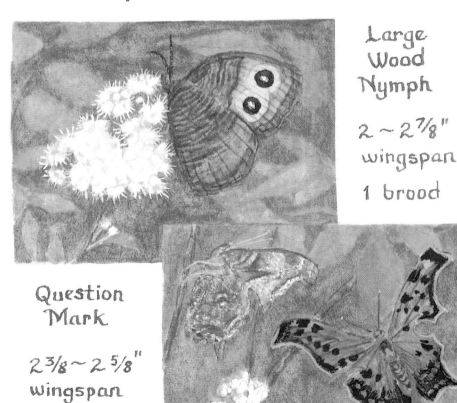

Large
Wood
Nymph

2 ~ 2⅞"
wingspan

1 brood

Question
Mark

2⅜ ~ 2⅝"
wingspan

2 broods

August Mushrooms

Birch
Scaberstalk
7"

3"
Pretty Russula

Parasol
10"

Red-wine Milkcap 2"

Orange
Stump
Mushrooms
2"

135

8"
Rooting
Collybia

2½"
Redgill Webcap

Bitter Bolete 8"

3"
Orange Milkcap

Little
Wheel   1"
Mushrooms

August 12~

Before the fog had lifted early this morning, we noticed a number of Turkey Vultures perched with wings outspread in the mountain maples south of the garden.

Turkey Vultures are known for their efficient use of energy.

During the night, their temperature drops. In the morning, they spread their massive wings to gather warmth from the sun.

They also conserve energy sitting at their roost for days if the weather is bad. When it's good, they soar on thermals scanning the ground for carrion.

Their sensitive sense of smell leads them to food sources. They may be ugly, but they are invaluable for cleaning up decaying carcasses.

August 19~

A Pickerel Frog,
well-camouflaged, rested
next to the pond. Usually,
we surprise them, and they us.
When we walk around the pond, we hear
"splash!...splash!...splash!" as they disappear,
too fast for us to see or identify them.

August 24~

An Eastern Milk Snake was slithering
under bushes in front of the house when
we spotted it. They grow up to 52". This
one was probably three feet or more.

They feed on rodents, lizards, birds,
and other snakes (including rattlesnakes
and copperheads) by
coiling around their
prey and
suffocating
them.

2'

Pearly
Everlasting

3'
Joe-Pye-Weed

2'
Meadowsweet

2'
Boneset

2'
Steeplebush

4'
White
Snakeroot

August __

1 – 5 PM: Heavy rain/thunderstorm followed by a complete rainbow. Watched a Fawn drink from the stream.

4 – 75°. The Belted Kingfisher flew all around pond proclaiming his ownership. On the way back uphill, twin Fawns watched my progress. The Doe, 50 yards higher, snorted and they ran for cover.

10 – The "Hav-a-Hart" trap in the fenced-in garden caught a Raccoon which we relocated.

12 – 92°, hazy, hot, humid. Early AM: 7 Turkey Vultures were drying their wings in tall trees south of the garden.

13 – Light rain. 8 PM: 2 sets of Doe with twin Fawns came out of woods below.

14 – 90°. Cedar Waxwings down by stream; a large Bullfrog sat motionless by pond. 7:30 PM: Watched 2 Does and 2 Fawns eating fallen apples. A big Dragonfly secured our area of mosquitoes.

15 – Misadventures with a White-tailed Buck and a Great Blue Heron. The Buck followed me as I tried to take photos of the Heron. Photo ops foiled by wrong camera lens.

16 – 80°. Wild Blackberries ripe for picking. Dead Fawn on road near big Beech tree. Cardinals and Cedar Waxwings at stream.

19 – 72°, sunny. Chickadees now showing up for niger seed. Many Grasshoppers in fields. At pond, a Pickerel Frog was well camouflaged in the foliage.

20 – 70°, clear. Saw many yellow birds (?) fly in and out of Blueberries.

21 – Cloudy, muggy. An Ovenbird crashed into porch window and died. Saw a male Scarlet Tanager in the Blueberries.

22 – Hung another Hummingbird feeder on other side of house. Now we have 4 Ruby-throated Hummingbirds fighting and zooming all around the house.

24 – At feeders: 4 Goldfinches all day; Doves, Cardinals, Nuthatches, Chickadees, and underneath – Chipmunks. Under bushes in front of house: an Eastern Milk Snake.

25 – Foggy AM, partly sunny PM, 60-70°. Saw Green Heron by pond.

26 – Red Damselflies flying in tandem laying eggs in pond. Saw 4-5 pairs at stream and 6-7 at pond. Red-spotted Purple Butterfly was drinking from pond.

28 – Heavy rain. Female Cardinal making frequent trips to feeders and Blueberries. Female Scarlet Tanager also in Blueberries.

30 – Evening Deer Watch: First to show up under Apple trees were 2 Bucks, a Doe and a Fawn. From the S. woods – 2 Does and 2 Fawns. From the N. field – 1 Doe and 2 Fawns.

31 – 70°, sunny. Cardinals and their young were bathing in stream. I played a cassette of Owl calls from tent. It pulled in Crows, Blue Jays and Chickadees, all very angry! Turned it off in a hurry.

SEPTEMBER

Fall color begins
in the bottom of the valley near the stream
and wetlands with the bright reds and oranges
of red maples and hornbeams, the golds of the
birches and beeches, then spreading up the
hills in a mixture of colors from the sugar
maples, aspens, wild cherries, and finally
culminating with the oranges of the larches.

Red Maples
start turning
orange, crimson,
and wine red
around the
middle of
September.

The Red Maple displays red in every season.

In winter, the buds are red, opening in spring to clusters of red and orange flowers.

In summer, the leafstalk and leaf veins are red, as are the winged seeds.

In autumn, as chlorophyll withdraws, sometimes leaving green splotches, the leaves' reds and oranges are revealed in all their flaming glory.

American Hornbeam

The fruits are clusters of nutlets in pairs.

The trunks of American Hornbeams are spiraled with ridges that look like twisted muscle.

This is one of our favorite scenes of autumn — the rosy-reds of the Hornbeam overhanging the stream, splashes of terra-cotta in the background as red maples begin their transformation; and in the foreground, the golds and greens of goldenrods and ferns.

The wood of American Hornbeam is extremely hard, like that of Hop Hornbeam (Ironwood). It is sometimes called Blue Beech because of its similar smooth, blue-gray bark. However, it isn't a member of the beech family.

Sept. 7~

The Blue Jays are back!

Their loud, raucous calls precede them as they swoop onto the feeders.

Even when I discovered where they were nesting up on the secluded side of the valley, I saw only furtive movements, and heard nothing.

Recently, I spotted many of them in the white pine grove near the house. However, they made themselves invisible when I tried to take pictures.

September 24 ~

There was such a racket coming from the lower meadow, we hiked down to investigate. Twenty-five to thirty Blue Jays were in the trees creating a mighty uproar over something.

Two cats, courting in the middle of the meadow must have set them off. They hate owls, hawks, snakes, and cats!

Sept. 28 ~

Today, they spotted an owl in the wild cherry tree, and harassed it until it finally flew away.

Sept. 30 ~

The Jays have been cramming all the seeds they can get into their craws, then flying to various places to store them — under leaves, in the ground, and wedged into the bark of trees.

September 7~

This beautiful Eastern Black Swallowtail was resting on a water parsnip flower by the pond. It looks like a female; males have more yellow markings and less blue. It could be preparing to lay eggs since parsley, carrots and celery are food sources for the larvae.

The first caterpillars that hatch are spiny, black, and white in the middle. They go through several moults until about an inch long.

Then, after casting off their skin, they emerge without spines, and are green with black stripes and yellow spots. Also, they're now equipped with a defense: scent horns. They push these out when they're disturbed, and the foul odor emitted scares away would-be predators.

They overwinter as chrysalides.

September 30 ～

I think this Praying Mantis got stuck on the barn door's wet paint. Usually, they're well camouflaged on green foliage where they wait, front legs folded as if in prayer, ready to pounce on other insects.

They are not only skilled predators, they are cannibals! In the spring, when the eggs hatch, the nymphs eat one another. In the fall, after mating, the female is likely to devour the male.

September 30 ～

In autumn, the Wooly Bear is a familiar sight, seen crawling around searching for a safe place to hibernate.

They curl into a ball when disturbed.

Cocoons are formed in spring and summer. The second generation larvae hibernate.

Isabella Tiger Moths emerge, seldom seen because they only fly at night.

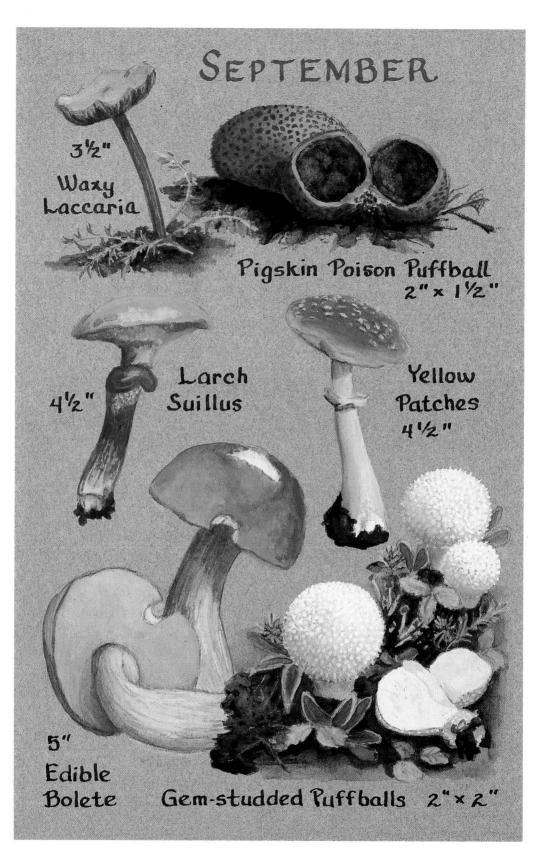

SEPTEMBER

3½"
Waxy
Laccaria

Pigskin Poison Puffball
2" x 1½"

4½"

Larch
Suillus

Yellow
Patches
4½"

5"
Edible
Bolete

Gem-studded Puffballs 2" x 2"

FUNGI

Pear-shaped Puffballs
1½" × 1½"

Shaggy
Mane

5"

6½"w.
Fleecy
Milkcap

Boletus
Calopus

4½"

Boletus
Luridus

4"

Boletus
Miniato-
olivaceus

4½"

September
12~

The Cardinals have started to bring their fledglings to the feeders.

This year the female is feeding a male and a female.

The fledgling phase is 3-4 weeks.

This is when we see them.

When the male brings his charge ~ a male fledgling~

he chases the others away, relegating them to the ground or nearby shrubs.

The nestling phase was 9-10 days.

This is when we heard them.

During the last three years, we've watched the male feed a young male while the female took care of two females, and one year – a male and a female.

The year before that, when only two survived, the male fed a female, and the female fed a male fledgling.

Calico
Aster

1-5'

1-3'

Daisy Fleabane

New
England
Aster
3-7'

Whorled
Wood
Aster
1-3'

Rush
Aster

3-8'

1-3'

Panicled Aster

Crooked
Stem
Aster

1-3'

2-7'

Purple-stemmed
Aster

Migrating Warblers

Magnolia Warbler
(Immature)

Tennessee
Warbler
(Female)

Cape May
Warbler
(Female)

September 20~25

Fortunately, the dogwood shrub next to the dining room window attracts insect-eating birds migrating through here in the spring and fall. Otherwise, it's impossible to get photos in the low growth around the woods where we get occasional glimpses of them. They flit too quickly for the camera, and are very reclusive.

Magnolia Warbler

Migrates from Canadian coniferous forests to Central and South America.
They don't have the sweet tooth the other two have. They eat some fruit, but mostly consume insects.

Tennessee Warbler

Migrates from boggy, swampy areas in Canada and northern United States to southern Mexico and northern South America.
Diet consists of insects with some berries, and in the winter some nectar.

Cape May Warbler

Migrates from coniferous forests in Canada to southern Florida and the West Indies.
These birds feed heavily on nectar during winter, and sometimes dip into grapes on the way down south, but chiefly eat insects.

SEPTEMBER ~

2 ~ 40° AM, 80° PM. The Blue Heron flew off when I was halfway down to the pond. The Green Heron remained in a tree.

4 ~ Heavy rain all day ~ 1½".

6 ~ 65°, partly cloudy. 7:30 PM: 10 Deer (4 Bucks among them) crossed from N. to S. field. 2 Does and 2 Fawns under apple trees again.

7 ~ 74°, sunny. Noisy Blue Jays back at feeders again. At pond: Eastern Black Swallowtail Butterfly, red Dragonflies.

9 ~ Next to Blue Jays, Crows and Crickets make the most noise now. Bats can be seen flying in the evening. Red Maple and American Hornbeam leaves turning red. Goldenrod and Aster flowers blooming everywhere.

11 ~ A flock of Goldfinches are busy eating spruce cone seeds. Cardinal family in maples above pond; Eastern Kingbirds by stream.

12 ~ Cardinal family at feeders: this year, the mother is feeding a male and a female. The father feeds a young male. It varies from year to year.

14 ~ 70°, clear. More trees turning color. Startled by a Common Garter Snake while picking carrots.

17 ~ Cold and drizzly. Much action at feeders: Purple and House Finches, Goldfinches, Blue Jays, Doves, Chickadees, Nuthatches, and the 5 Cardinals.

18 ~ 32° AM, 60° PM. Deer already have darker coats. Great Blue Heron still at pond. Red Dragonflies and Damselflies still active.

20~ Warblers in dogwood shrub eating insects from under leaves. Sugar Maples turning golden.

24~ 32° 7 AM, 50° 2 PM. Yellow-bellied Flycatcher in Blue Spruce. 25-30 Blue Jays created a ruckus over 2 cats in meadow.

26~ Cold and rainy yesterday; foggy AM. Multi-colored leaves scattered over lower hemlocks make them look like decorated Christmas trees. A mist hovered over pond... reflections of fall colors on water surreally gorgeous!

27~ Overcast, 50° A Cottontail Rabbit browses in the front yard, oblivious to our comings and goings.

28~ 28° AM, frost on ground. Blue Jays harrassed an Owl in a Black Cherry tree until it flew away. Still a few Dragonflies at pond.

29~ Our neighbour reported seeing many deer in their alfalfa field and evidence of a bear in their corn field. That news and a spectacular sunset drew me to the woods across the road after supper. Mesmerized by the brilliant colors behind the mountains, I almost missed seeing the Black Bear. It was standing upright, gorging on the corn, about a hundred feet away. The Bear saw me; I saw the Bear. He or she turned back to the corn, as I did to the sunset.

30~ 60° sunny. Blue Jays have been emptying the feeders and storing seeds everywhere. Found a Praying Mantis stuck to wet paint on barn door. Wooly Bear Caterpillars are seen frequently now.

OCTOBER

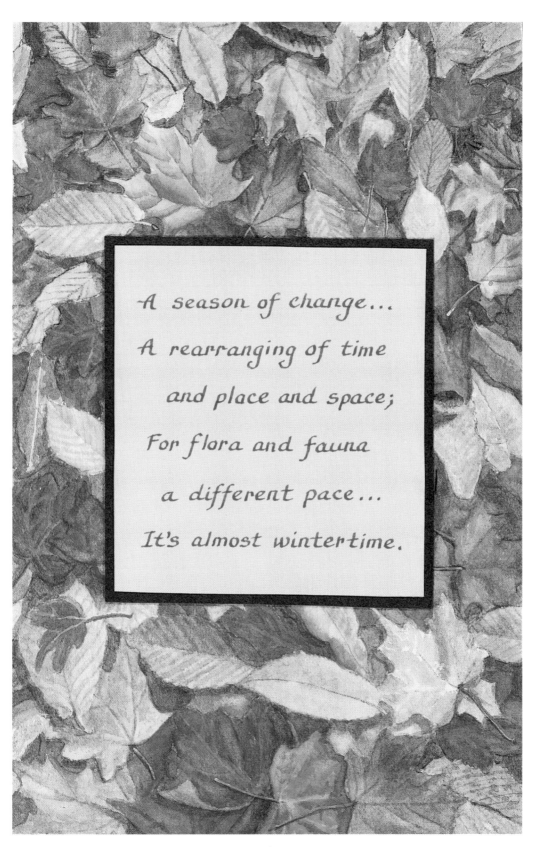

A season of change...
A rearranging of time
   and place and space;
For flora and fauna
   a different pace...
It's almost wintertime.

Sugar Maples

The glorious Sugar Maples now take center stage. The scarlet foliage of red maples has faded. The aspen leaves pictured on the left above are still green, but that too will soon change. Gradually, fall color is creeping up the mountain.

Sugar Maples are famous for maple syrup made from its sap; and furniture, flooring and cabinets made from its wood.

The winged, paired seeds mature and are released in autumn.

Sugar Maple
Leaves

Common Milkweed

The pods on these Milkweed plants were still closed in early October. Even though an individual plant will produce as many as 600 flowers, only 4-6 of them will mature into pods. Pollination is tricky; many insects get stuck and can't carry pollen to another milkweed.

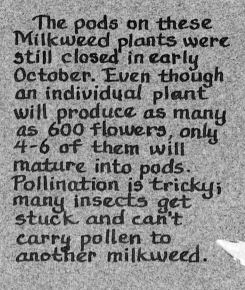

October 18 ~ Today the pods split open. The seeds, attached to feathery "parachutes," gradually loosen and float off with the wind.

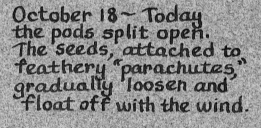

Yellow-bellied Flycatcher

October 1 ~

A few days ago, I saw a Yellow-bellied Flycatcher in the spruces just long enough to identify. Today, it came within camera range on the porch railing.

They hide in the damp undergrowth of conifers, eating ants and beetles.

The only areas where they nest in Pennsylvania are the Pocono Mountains and northern spruce forests, which we offer.

Woodchuck (Groundhog)   October 3 ~

This Woodchuck, waddling across our lawn, has really put on weight since we first saw him or her in March.

Woodchucks start denning up in October, and will hibernate until February or March. They live over winter on their own body fat.

Body temperatures drop from 90° to below 50° Heartbeats slow down from over 100 beats a minute to only four.

↑Yellow Birch   Gray Birch↑   Aspen↑

Circling the pond are Yellow Birches, Gray Birches, and a few Aspens. It's no surprise for these "pioneer" trees to take root here. This was a hemlock forest until twelve years ago when the hemlocks became a barn, and dredging brought forth a pond. Pioneer trees, like these, are the first to spring up in cut-over lands.

Gray Birches are short-lived, often broken by snow, ice and rainstorms. Yellow Birches, however, can grow to a height of 100 feet; and so far, those around the pond and stream have not been overtaken by the hemlocks.

The Aspens, near the pond and halfway up the hill, are doomed. Beavers keep gnawing them down to eat their inner bark and to use the poles to construct their dams.

169

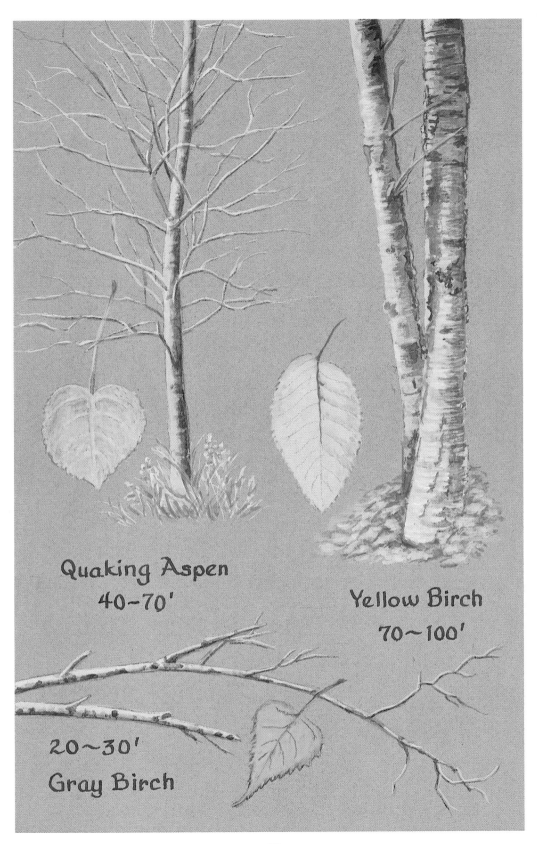

Quaking Aspen
40~70'

Yellow Birch
70~100'

20~30'
Gray Birch

October 3 — Father Cardinal is still feeding Junior. Mother Cardinal has the male in her charge eating by himself, but she still feeds Sister.

These young birds are gradually gaining color, particularly the males who are darkening around the beak and eyes. All three young birds still have gray beaks.

October 18 —
Now they're all able to feed themselves.

Sister is the only one to announce her presence by "chipping" when she lands on the feeder. We hear the others "chip" in the bushes before they approach the feeders.

October 31 — We haven't seen the young birds lately, just the adults when they come to the feeders.

We watched the parents putting pressure on each fledgling to leave as soon as it could feed itself.

They were obviously successful in launching another generation!

October 6 ～ For the past week we have been hearing a racket in the woods across the road. It sounds as if someone is pruning the high spruce branches: first a cracking sound, then a thud. The evidence of squirrel activity is the huge mound of Norway spruce cones shown below.

We don't know which squirrel is harvesting the cones ～ the Red or the Gray Squirrel. The Red is the feistiest. The Gray is more reclusive, but shows up frequently near the bird-feeders.

Tail: 8～10"

8～11"

Gray Squirrel

Red Squirrel
  7½ - 8½"
 Tail:
  4 - 6"

October 10 ~ Evidence of another sort was
noted today down by the stream. In several
places the bark of small branches has been
stripped: "buck rubbing."

By the beginning of rut season, the velvet
on a buck's antlers has died. Bucks peel it
off by rubbing against saplings and
branches.

They also engage the branches in mock
combat to prepare themselves for competition
during breeding season.

American Beech

Our Beech trees are interspersed among the maples and hemlocks.

Beechnuts mature in autumn and split into four parts.

They provide food for mice and squirrels, bears and raccoons, turkeys and grouse.

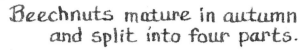

Northern Red Oak

This is the only oak to grow at our northeastern Pennsylvania altitude.

A sprouting acorn develops full-sized leaves. The leaves on this Red Oak sapling are 8" long!

It takes almost 20 years for oak trees to bear acorns, and two years for a Red Oak acorn to mature.

Wild Black Cherry

Numerous
Wild Black Cherry
trees grow between
our backyard and the
meadows. The tallest
tree affords birds a
vantage point to
assess our area;
and offers us
a chance to
assess them!

The wood is used
for furniture; the bark
is turned into cough syrup;
the cherries are made into wine and jelly.

October___

1 – 55°, windy. Male Goldfinches' bright yellow feathers turning gray. Yellow-bellied Flycatcher rested briefly on back porch railing. Fall foliage gorgeous!

3 – 50°, cloudy. Cardinals still feeding 2 of their young. One of the male fledglings is eating on his own. A fat Woodchuck waddled across lawn this afternoon.

4 – Overcast. Loud honking of Canadian Geese drew us outside to see their V-formation at tree level as they headed south.

5 – 60's, sunny, cold winds. Many Robins on lawn and bushes. Trees at base of mountains and Red Maples losing their leaves. Sugar Maples are gloriously golden!

6 – Gray Squirrels and/or Red Squirrels are making a racket harvesting Spruce cones across the road. There's a new Woodchuck burrow next to path across road.

8 – 30°AM, 54°PM. Early evening: we counted 10 Deer in high meadow, 5 in Big Red's field, and 10 in our fields.

9 – 50's, sunny. Have been hearing 5 or more flocks of Geese heading south daily. Birch, Beech, Aspen leaves now turning golden. Saw Blue Heron at south stream.

10 – 20° 7AM, 40° noon, windy. Dark-eyed Juncos have returned. Belted Kingfisher still at pond. Scraped tree branches next to stream evidence of Bucks rubbing velvet off their antlers.

12 — Monarch Butterflies still here feeding on flowers. Black Cherry trees now turning yellow.

13 — 70°, sunny. Flies, Wasps, Daddy-long-legs, Ladybugs all trying to get into house. Still some red Damselflies at pond.

16 — 70's, "Indian Summer"; lovely breeze PM. Milkweed pods are opening and scattering seeds to the winds.

18 — All 3 Cardinal fledglings come to the feeders by themselves now.

22 — Snow flurries. Goldfinches and Downy Woodpecker at niger seed feeder.

26 — 30° 7 AM. Snow flurries until 2 PM. At feeders: Goldfinches, Chickadees, Blue Jays, Nuthatches, Cardinals, Juncos and a female Downy Woodpecker. Blue Jays scared away a huge bird in the Black Cherry tree.

28 — 20° - 45°, heavy rain. A Fox Sparrow showed up at feeders.

30 — 16° 7 AM; frost on ground. Larch trees' needles have turned orange. Pond has thin skin of ice.

31 — Partly sunny, cold. PM: A real Halloween night sky. A half-moon would be covered by drifting dark clouds, then suddenly reappear illuminating the orange Larch trees. We didn't see any bats flying... but we know they're there.

NOVEMBER

We live from
One breath to another
On the verge of nothingness,
Believing life is ours forever,
Acting our parts most earnestly,
Ad libbing to suit our whims and egos,
Charging and whirling through our days,
As though there is escape in movement
From the fear of the inevitable.

Yet there are those who have known
The ecstasy of eternity
In a quiet moment —
Between one breath and another —
When the full beauty of being
Is understood.
 — Bernie

The last burst of autumn color comes from Tamarack or Larch trees. The only other colors are greens of conifers and fields plus the ochres of dry leaves and weeds.

November is really bleak after the Tamaracks have shed their needles. They are true conifers, bearing needles and cones, but, strangely enough, are also deciduous.

Maybe they evolved that way to survive the frigid zones of Canada. The Tamarack grows farther north in North America than any other tree.

This is one of 3 Apple Trees left from an orchard planted many years ago. It still produces apples, too tart to eat from the tree, but great for cooking.

The deer aren't so fussy. They come in droves when the fruit ripens, starting in late August and lasting through September.

It's a popular place at twilight for does to bring their fawns. That's when we bring out the binoculars to watch fawns chase each other around this island of trees, and observe does and bucks standing on their hind legs to reach the apples.

November 14 —

From the upper level of our house, I had been watching a doe foraging in the snowy fields. Soon a buck ventured out of the woods.

This is the rutting (breeding) season. Among Whitetail Deer in Pennsylvania, this lasts from late October through December.

Does become receptive to males for only a 24-30 hour period. She will mate only during that time.

The doe obviously wasn't ready. But the buck wasn't taking any chances of this doe getting away, and lay down close by to keep an eye on her.

If fertilization does not occur, the doe will come into heat (estrus) again 28 days later. Opportunities last for 3 cycles usually.

Once bred, the birth of fawns will follow in about 205 days.

I opened the window extremely carefully; but the slight noise was enough to alert the buck who stood up, ears cocked to discern if danger existed nearby.

All breeding age bucks try to court does; but the largest buck is the one who follows a doe closely, feeds and beds with her, and is on hand to mate when she is ready.

The dominant buck probably breeds most of the does close by.

While the buck was staring up at me, the doe slipped away. He looked left and right; then nose to ground, followed the scent to find her again.

Red
Maple
60~90'

Gray
Birch
20~30'

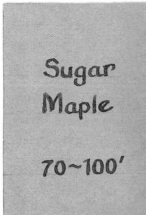

Sugar
Maple

70~100'

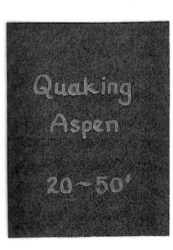

Quaking
Aspen

20~50'

Cardinals

Nov. 1~ 2 Cardinals, 3 Blue
Jays, 6 Juncos

3~ 1 Downy Woodpecker
at suet feeder

4~ 13 Pine Siskins fighting
over niger seed

5~ 1st snowfall. 2 Cardinals,
3 Blue Jays, Chickadees,
Nuthatches, Pine Siskins,
Juncos and Woodpecker

10~ A male Goldfinch joined
the other birds.

11~ 5" of snow by afternoon

12~ 12 Evening Grosbeaks
dropped in for ½ hour.

Pine
Siskin

House
Sparrow

Junco

Evening

Nuthatch

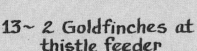

At the Feeders

Blue Jay

13~ 2 Goldfinches at thistle feeder

14~ 5° at 7 AM. Goldfinches and House Sparrows plus regulars

15~ Pine Siskins are back.

19- 8-12" of snow during night. Cardinals, Blue Jays, Chickadees, Downy Woodpecker, Nuthatches, House Sparrows, Juncos, and this time ~ two dozen Evening Grosbeaks

25~ Snow has all melted.

Goldfinch

Chickadee

Grosbeaks

Downy Woodpecker

DECEMBER

Mount Ararat

I do not speak of Noah or the Ark,
but of the mountain which is our backyard,
that summer greenclothed
bulge of earth and stone.

I've always loved the mountain's wooded crown,
its pure, majestic forest where the game
live as they did before the Long Knives came.

Now they've built a tower on its summit
with blinking lights to make the stars submit;
and crimson laser beams to pierce the skies
to lure migrating birds to their demise.

I sadly wonder why God trusted man
and gave to him such power of dominion,
yet failed to train him, teach him due respect
for His great skill as landscape architect.

                           — Bernie

December 2 ~

Today we counted 19 Wild Turkeys emerging from the woods. There was a heavy snowfall last night. They must be very hungry to leave their cover. We frequently hear them, but can never find them. The illustrations below are based on long-distance photography. They are more wary of humans than deer are.

Wild Turkeys have keen hearing and eyesight, and are clever at hiding. If flushed, they can fly short distances at 40-55 mph, or run at 18 mph. If we come upon them unexpectedly, they usually fly.

Wild Turkeys almost became extinct in the 19th century from heavy hunting and loss of habitat. Now, due to careful game management, their numbers have come back.

They need large trees for night roosting, and ground cover for nesting and rearing their young. In warm weather they need fruits, grains, insects, spiders, snails, etc. In winter they need seeds, nuts and acorns.

Wild Turkeys

Wild Turkeys are slimmer than domesticated turkeys, have longer legs and necks, and smaller heads. Adult males, called "gobblers" or "toms," weigh up to 25 pounds. Hens are shorter and weigh 9-10 pounds. The plumage of Wild Turkeys is much more iridescent, glowing with copper, green, bronze and purple in sunlight.

The gobbler is famous for his spectacular courtship display in spring when he struts and gobbles, spreads his tail, swells his wattles and rattles his wings. If a rival male shows up, a fight will ensue. The victor wins a harem of hens, from 3-5 to a dozen or more.

Because hens nest on the ground, they, their eggs and their young are easy prey for predators. Nest-building, incubation and care of the young are done entirely by the female. The chicks, called "poults," become strong fliers by 5-6 weeks of age, and are almost self-sufficient by the end of summer.

Dark-eyed Juncos, also called "snowbirds," flock to feeders during bad winter weather. They prefer feeding on the ground. Winter flocks range from 10~30 birds. They start appearing here in October.

There are 5 regional variations of this species, formerly regarded as separate species. (The distinct color differences confused the issue.) The Juncos we see in the east are Slate-colored Juncos. The others are the Oregon Junco in the west, the Pink-sided Junco in the central Rockies, the Gray-headed Junco in the southern Rockies, and the White-winged Junco in the Black Hills. They interbreed where their ranges overlap.

All Juncos have pink bills and white outer tail feathers that flash off and on as they fan their tails in flight.

Here in Pennsylvania, they breed in the higher mountains. The female incubates 4-5 eggs on the ground. After nesting, they join mixed-species flocks and go south or into lowland areas.

Dark-eyed Juncos

Nuthatch pairs remain together in the same area year-round. The name evolved from "nuthack," since they wedge nuts into crevices, then hack them open. They prefer coming down tree trunks headfirst as they forage for insects and insect eggs under the bark.

The two we see are Whitebreasted Nut-hatches. They come to the feeders for seeds and suet, and carry off more than they can eat, which they store in loose bark (or shingles and walls).

Courtship begins in late winter with mate-feeding continuing into April. 5-8 eggs are laid in a nest located in a tree cavity. Food is stored near the nest for easy access for the male to feed the brooding female. The young are fed insects and other animal food by both parents.

In winter, the male and female roost in separate tree cavities. They forage with other species, such as chickadees and downy woodpeckers.

White-breasted Nuthatches

Blue Jays plummet down to our feeders screeching like hawks, which frightens all the other birds away. They cram as many seeds as they can into their bills and throat pouch; then fly away to eat, or bury the seeds to eat later.

Besides intimidating other birds, Blue Jays have a bad reputation as nest robbers, eating birds' eggs and nestlings.

On the plus side, their cache of seeds and acorns, stuck in the ground or bark of trees, helps reforestation, and gives provender for small animals in winter. Blue Jays also serve as sentinels, alerting birds and other creatures to intruders, including us, with shrill, raucous cries.

They make other calls which are surprisingly soft: low whistles, whispers, and soft notes during courtship and breeding.

Six Blue

They become quiet and furtive during nesting season. This is when they disappear from our view. We finally found them on the opposite slope, far removed from human habitation. A nest of twigs and grass will hold 3-7 eggs. The male feeds the brooding female and later the baby birds.

Parents and young stay together through the summer, long past the fledgling phase. In the fall, they join other family groups and explore in large noisy flocks. Some of the Blue Jays then migrate south, mostly 1st-year birds. Adults stay within the same area.

Winter groups average 4-6 birds. At winter feeders, Blue Jays prefer sunflower seeds, suet and peanuts. At other seasons they're omnivorous.

Jays

December 5— South Field   36°

A doe has been bringing her fawns up from the woods, past our barn, across the road, and onto our neighbor's fields (where corn, alfalfa and clover are grown in the summer.)

In the spring and summer, Whitetail Deer consume weeds, grains, grasses, clover, wildflowers, mushrooms, green leaves and new growth on woody plants. Leaves and stems are eaten throughout the year. In the fall, apples and acorns are their favorites, followed by corn, pears and cherries. Evergreen leaves, hard browse and dry leaves are winter's menu.

Fawns lose their spotted coats by the end of September. By late autumn, they are about two-thirds the size of their mothers. Then growth stops until springtime so that nutrients can be converted to fat, essential to survival.

December 16 — North Field   42°

This could be the same doe with fawns, or another doe family. There must be many such groups due to our large deer population.

Their habitat here is ideal: abundant woods for protection, forest edges and farmers' fields for browsing and grazing, the stream for water, and hills on both sides to deflect winter winds.

The most common social group of Whitetail Deer is an adult doe, her fawns and her yearling female offspring. Sometimes 3 or 4 generations of related does live together. Adult and yearling bucks form small groups (2-4 animals) which stay together except during breeding season when they separate. After that, large mixed groups form during feeding periods, and break into subgroups for bedding.

INDEX

BIRDS

MAMMALS

REPTILES, AMPHIBIANS AND FISH

BUTTERFLIES AND MOTHS

DAMSELFLIES AND DRAGONFLIES

INSECTS AND SPIDERS

WILDFLOWERS

TREES AND SHRUBS

NON-FLOWERING PLANTS

FUNGI